FEB 21 2013

D1544973

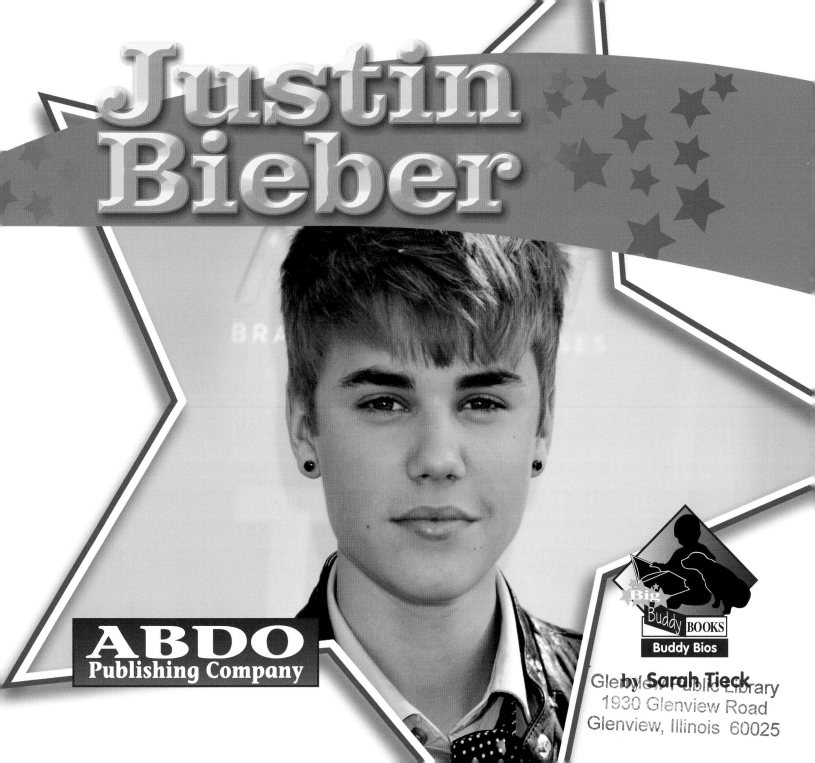

Justin Bieber

ABDO
Publishing Company

Big Buddy BOOKS
Buddy Bios

by Sarah Tieck

Glenview Public Library
1930 Glenview Road
Glenview, Illinois 60025

VISIT US AT
www.abdopublishing.com

Published by ABDO Publishing Company, PO Box 398166, Minneapolis, MN 55439.

Copyright © 2012 by Abdo Consulting Group, Inc. International copyrights reserved in all countries. No part of this book may be reproduced in any form without written permission from the publisher. Big Buddy Books™ is a trademark and logo of ABDO Publishing Company.

Printed in the United States of America, North Mankato, Minnesota.
102011
052012
 PRINTED ON RECYCLED PAPER

Coordinating Series Editor: Rochelle Baltzer
Contributing Editors: Megan M. Gunderson, BreAnn Rumsch, Marcia Zappa
Graphic Design: Maria Hosley
Cover Photograph: *AP Photo*: Gregg DeGuire/PictureGroup via AP IMAGES.
Interior Photographs/Illustrations: *AP Photo*: AP Photo (p. 25), AP Photo, file (p. 25), Evan Agostini (pp. 21, 25), Vince Buccil/MTV/PictureGroup via AP IMAGES (p. 29), The Canadian Press, Darren Calabrese (p. 5), Mark Davis/PictureGroup via AP IMAGES (p. 26), Scott Gries/Picture Group via AP Images (p. 9), Manny Hernandez/Picture Group via AP Images (p. 9), Peter Kramer/NBC NewsWire via AP Images (p. 29), Matt Sayles (p. 27); *Getty Images*: Craig Barritt (p. 13), Bryan Bedder (p. 15), Jeff Kravitz/FilmMagic, Inc. (p. 11), Kevin Mazur/WireImage (p. 22), George Pimentel/WireImage (p. 7), Craig Sjodin/Disney Channel via Getty Images (p. 17), Kevin Winter/Getty Images Entertainment (p. 18).

Library of Congress Cataloging-in-Publication Data

Tieck, Sarah, 1976-
 Justin Bieber : pop music superstar / Sarah Tieck.
   p. cm. -- (Big buddy biographies)
  ISBN 978-1-61783-224-6
 1. Bieber, Justin, 1994---Juvenile literature. 2. Singers--Canada--Biography--Juvenile literature. I. Title.
 ML3930.B54T53 2012
 782.42164092--dc23
 [B]
                              2011037820

Contents

Music Star. 4

Family Ties 6

Starting Out 8

Big Break 10

First Album 12

A Singer's Life 16

Catching On 20

Fan Fever 24

Off the Stage 26

Buzz 28

Snapshot 30

Important Words 31

Web Sites 31

Index 32

Did you know...

Some of Justin's fans call him JBiebs.

Justin is also famous for his style. Fans were surprised when he cut his hair in early 2011!

Music Star

Justin Bieber is a talented singer. He is best known for singing popular music. Fans around the world love his albums and songs.

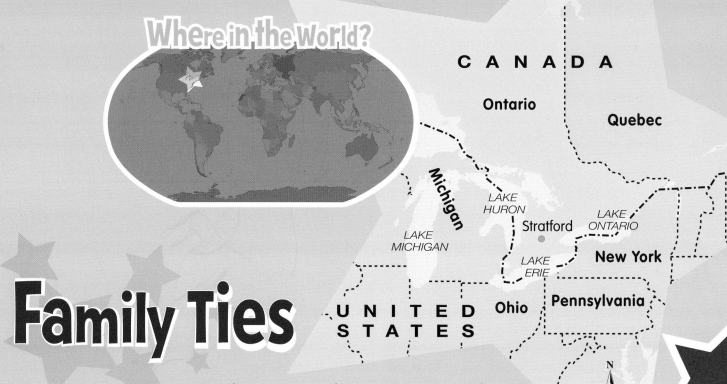

Where in the World?

CANADA

Ontario

Quebec

Michigan

LAKE HURON

LAKE MICHIGAN

Stratford

LAKE ONTARIO

LAKE ERIE

New York

UNITED STATES

Ohio

Pennsylvania

N W E S

Family Ties

Justin Drew Bieber was born in Stratford, Ontario, Canada, on March 1, 1994. His parents are Jeremy Bieber and Pattie Mallette.

Justin's parents separated when he was young. His mother raised him in Stratford. There, Justin attended school and was a good student.

Growing up, Justin did not see his dad very often. Yet, they have grown closer over the years.

BIEBER NEVER

Jazmyn, Jeremy, and Pattie sometimes attend events with Justin.

Did you know...

Justin has a younger half sister named Jazmyn and a half brother named Jaxon.

Starting Out

From a young age, Justin was a talented singer. When he was 12, he entered a local singing contest. He earned second place!

Family and friends wanted to see Justin **perform**. So in 2007, he and his mom began to post videos on a Web site called YouTube. That way, people could watch him sing wherever they were.

Justin has always loved music.
He taught himself to play drums,
piano, guitar, and trumpet.

Big Break

Millions of people saw Justin **perform** on YouTube. Music **executives** noticed his talent and wanted him to make an album. In 2008, Justin signed a deal to record music.

Soon, Justin and his mom moved to Atlanta, Georgia. There, Justin was closer to his work. He began to record pop and **rhythm and blues** songs for his first album. He also worked with private teachers to keep up with school.

Did you know...

Famous singer Justin Timberlake also wanted to work with Justin. But, Justin decided to work with Usher instead.

Justin became friends with famous singer Usher (*left*). Usher helped Justin record his own music. Later they recorded music together.

First Album

Justin worked hard to record songs and videos for his album. He **released** four songs before the album came out. These singles were "One Time," "One Less Lonely Girl," "Love Me," and "Favorite Girl."

Fans became very excited about these songs. They were hits before Justin's album even came out! This rarely happens for new artists.

Justin is a skilled dancer. He shows off his talent in music videos and onstage.

Did you know...

Justin wrote the song "Where Are You Now" about missing his dad.

Justin travels around the United States and Canada to perform. He has also performed in Europe, Asia, Australia, and South America.

Did you know...

Justin has performed for the US president! He said it was exciting to meet President Obama and his family.

In November 2009, Justin **released** his first album. It is called *My World*. It sold many copies during its first week. Within two months, it went platinum. This means it sold more than 1 million copies!

A Singer's Life

As a singer, Justin spends time practicing his songs. He works with people in the music business to improve his sound. They often work together in recording studios, where albums are made.

Justin has been a guest on many radio stations, such as Radio Disney.

Did you know...

Justin often wears a dog tag necklace. This was a gift from a fan.

Did you know...

Justin has a dog named Sam.
He also has a pet snake.

18

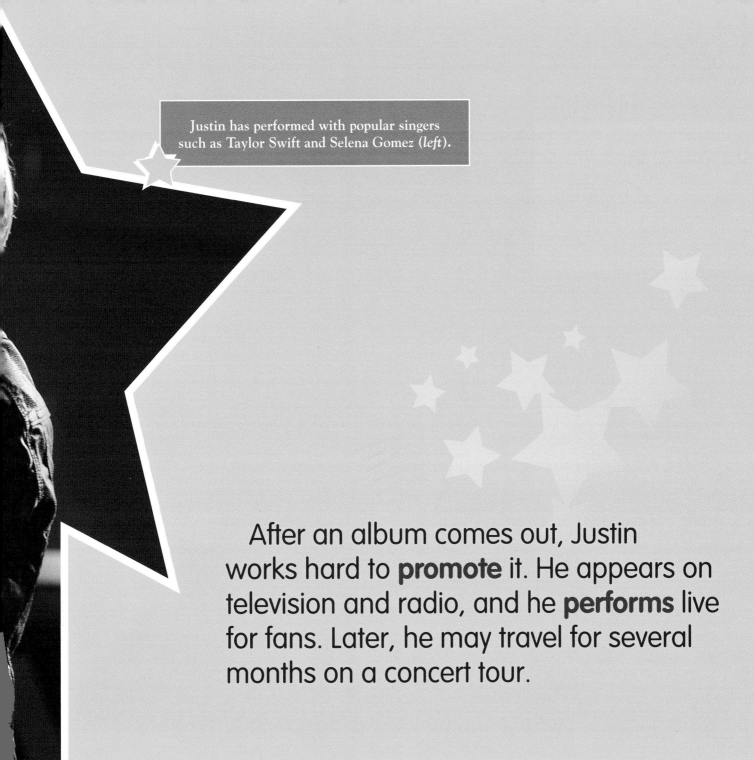

Justin has performed with popular singers such as Taylor Swift and Selena Gomez *(left)*.

After an album comes out, Justin works hard to **promote** it. He appears on television and radio, and he **performs** live for fans. Later, he may travel for several months on a concert tour.

Did you know...

People have compared Justin to famous 1960s singer Stevie Wonder. Both found success at a young age.

In summer 2010, Justin started his first major concert tour. The My World Tour promoted his first two albums.

Catching On

In March 2010, *My World 2.0* was released. Justin's second album was an even bigger hit than his first one! The songs "Baby" and "Somebody to Love" were especially popular.

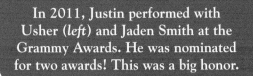

In 2011, Justin performed with Usher (*left*) and Jaden Smith at the Grammy Awards. He was nominated for two awards! This was a big honor.

Did you know...

Justin released an album of songs with his movie. It is called *Never Say Never: The Remixes*. The songs feature other famous singers such as Miley Cyrus, Jaden Smith, and Usher.

A 3-D movie about Justin's life came out in February 2011. *Justin Bieber: Never Say Never* told the story of how Justin became a famous singer. It includes videos from his life and from backstage at his concerts. The movie was a hit!

Fan Fever

Over the years, many music artists have become very popular. Some couldn't even walk down the street because fans got so excited. These stars include Elvis Presley, the Beatles, the Jackson Five, and New Kids on the Block.

Like these **performers**, Justin has very excited fans. Early in his career, about 3,000 fans came to a shopping mall to meet him!

Thousands of fans want to meet Justin and see him perform.

John Lennon, Ringo Starr, Paul McCartney, and George Harrison were in the Beatles (*above*). In the 1960s, Beatles fans (*left*) were so excited to meet them, police had to keep control.

In 2010, Justin began dating Selena Gomez. Their fans were very interested in this news!

Off the Stage

When Justin is not working, he spends time with his family and friends. He likes to dance and go out on dates. And he has fun making jokes. Justin also enjoys spending time online.

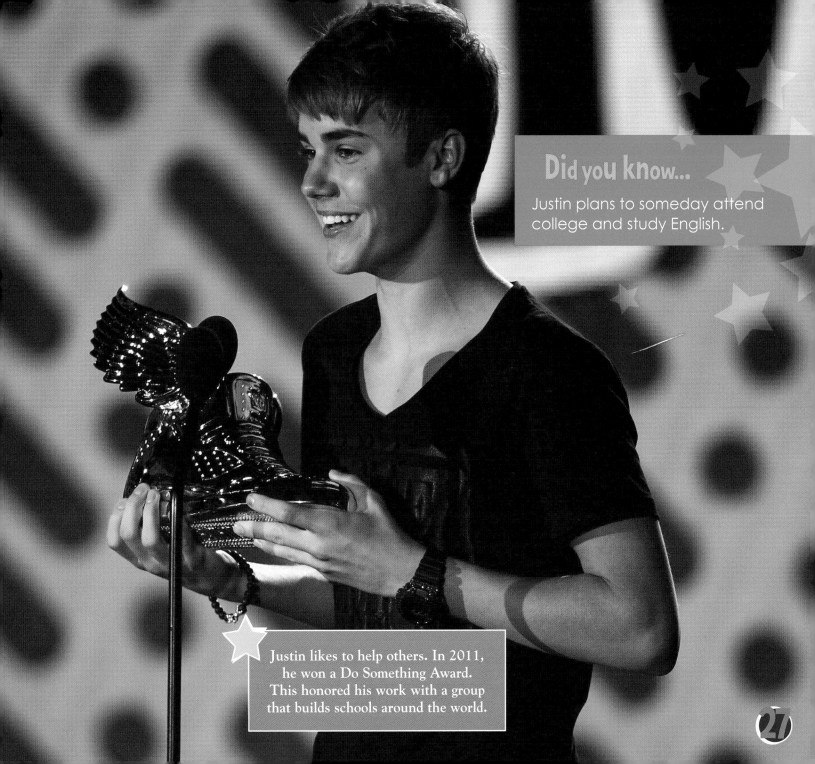

Did you know...

Justin plans to someday attend college and study English.

Justin likes to help others. In 2011, he won a Do Something Award. This honored his work with a group that builds schools around the world.

Did you know...

One of Justin's favorite colors is purple. He often wears colorful sneakers. He especially likes high-tops.

Reporters often take Justin's picture. And, fans ask for his picture and autograph.

Buzz

In late 2011, Justin **released** a holiday album. It is called *Under the Mistletoe*. Fans were very excited to hear his new music!

Meanwhile, Justin's fame continues to grow. His work has been **nominated** for awards, and he has won many of them. Fans look forward to what's next for Justin Bieber! Many believe he has a bright **future**.

In 2011, Justin won an MTV Movie Award for *Justin Bieber: Never Say Never.*

Snapshot

★**Name**: Justin Drew Bieber

★**Birthday**: March 1, 1994

★**Birthplace**: Stratford, Ontario, Canada

★**Albums**: *My World, My World 2.0, Never Say Never: The Remixes, Under the Mistletoe*

★**Appearance**: *Justin Bieber: Never Say Never*

Important Words

executive (ihg-ZEH-kyuh-tihv) a high-level employee who manages or directs a company.

future (FYOO-chuhr) a time that has not yet occurred.

nominate to name as a possible winner.

perform to do something in front of an audience.

promote to help something become known.

release to make available to the public.

rhythm (RIH-thuhm) **and blues** a form of popular music that features a strong beat. It is inspired by jazz, gospel, and blues styles.

Web Sites

To learn more about Justin Bieber, visit ABDO Publishing Company online. Web sites about Justin Bieber are featured on our Book Links page. These links are routinely monitored and updated to provide the most current information available.

www.abdopublishing.com

Index

awards **23, 27, 28, 29**

Beatles **24, 25**

Bieber, Jaxon **7, 26**

Bieber, Jazmyn **7, 26**

Bieber, Jeremy **6, 7, 13, 26**

Canada **6, 14, 30**

Cyrus, Miley **23**

education **6, 10, 27**

Georgia **10**

Gomez, Selena **19, 26**

Jackson Five **24**

Justin Bieber: Never Say Never (movie) **23, 29, 30**

Mallette, Pattie **6, 7, 8, 10, 26**

My World (album) **10, 12, 14, 20, 30**

My World 2.0 (album) **20, 30**

My World Tour **20**

Never Say Never: The Remixes (album) **23, 30**

New Kids on the Block **24**

Obama, Barack **14**

Presley, Elvis **24**

Radio Disney **17**

Smith, Jaden **23**

Swift, Taylor **19**

Timberlake, Justin **11**

Under the Mistletoe (album) **28, 30**

Usher **11, 23**

Wonder, Stevie **20**

YouTube **8, 10**

3 1170 00910 7669